THE
SCORPION

BY
JAN MELL

EDITED BY
JULIE BACH

CRESTWOOD HOUSE
New York

LIBRARY OF CONGRESS CATALOGING IN PUBLICATION DATA

Mell, Jan.
    The scorpion

    (Wildlife, habits & habitat)
    Includes index.
    SUMMARY: Examines the physical characteristics, behavior, and natural environ-
ment of the scorpion.
    1. Scorpions—Juvenile literature.   [1. Scorpions.]   I. Title.   II. Series.
QL458.7.M45   1990   595.4'6—dc20   89-28273
ISBN 0-89686-520-7

PHOTO CREDITS:

Cover: Photo Researchers: (Francois Gohier)
DRK Photo: (R.J. Erwin) 4; (Stephen J. Krasemann) 20, 30, 44-45; (M.P. Kahl) 24;
    (Stanley Breeden) 28-29; (Len Rue Jr.) 39; (C. Lockwood) 40
Journalism Services: (Dan Smith) 6
Photo Researchers: (Tom McHugh) 7, 9, 12, 15, 21, 31, 35, 36-37; (Anthony Merceica)
    10; (Jany Sauvanet) 17; (Ray Simons) 18; (Lawrence E. Naylor) 19; (Gilbert Grant)
    27; (Stephen Dalton) 32; (R.J. Erwin) 43

Macmillan Publishing Company
866 Third Avenue
New York, NY 10022
Collier Macmillan Canada, Inc.

Printed in the United States of America
First Edition
10 9 8 7 6 5 4 3 2 1

TABLE OF CONTENTS

As long as people have walked on the earth, they have feared scorpions. In ancient Egypt, scorpions were carved into monuments. Chants were spoken and sung to keep the creatures from harming people. During the fourteenth, fifteenth, and sixteenth centuries, scorpions were symbols of disloyalty and faithlessness.

In the days before scientific classification, people called any small, multilegged creature an insect. They believed that scorpions were insects, too. But the more scientists studied the scorpion, the more they found out about what it actually is and does.

Today, *entomologists* (people who study insects and scorpions) have labeled the scorpion an *arthropod*, not an insect. They have put the scorpion into the class *Arachnida*. Spiders, ticks, mites, centipedes, and daddy longlegs are also in this class. Scorpions belong to the order *Scorpionida*.

What frightens people most about scorpions is their poisonous sting. But scientists have learned that scorpions do not sting humans on purpose. They attack only when they are frightened. By carefully studying the scorpion, entomologists have learned a great deal about this arthropod.

For many years, people were afraid of scorpions. Today, scientists are learning more about this mysterious arthropod.

The cephalothorax and the abdomen are the two parts of a scorpion's body. The last six segments of the abdomen form the tail.

CHAPTER ONE:

Not an insect

Early scientists thought scorpions were insects because they have many of the same characteristics. Both animals have segmented bodies. Their shells are hard and must be shed as the animals grow. This is called *molting*. Both insects and scorpions have paired *appendages*. As scientists became more knowledgeable, however, they noticed differences between insects and scorpions. These differences placed the animals into separate classes and orders.

The body of the scorpion has two parts, the *cephalothorax* and the *abdomen*. The last six segments of the abdomen form the tail. At the end of the tail is the stinger. Insects, on the other hand, have three main body parts, the head, chest, and abdomen.

The scorpion has six pairs of jointed appendages. The first pair are tiny mouth pincers, called *chelicerae*. They act as jaws. The second pair are large arms called *pedipalps*, which have claws on the end. The claws are used to

The emperor scorpion, found in West Africa, is the world's largest scorpion.

catch food, or *prey*. Behind the pedipalps are four pairs of legs. Scorpions don't have antennae or feelers as insects do.

On the underside of the scorpion are several openings. The opening on the wide part of the scorpion is the *genital opening*. Beyond that opening are four pairs of holes called the *spiracles*. They bring air into the internal breathing organs, called *book lungs*.

Behind the genital opening, there is a pair of comblike organs called *pectines* that are used during mating. They are found only on scorpions. When a scorpion is at rest its pectines lay flat against its abdomen. When it walks, the pectines swing back and forth along the ground.

Scorpions vary in size and color. The largest can be eight inches long and are usually dark brown or black. The smallest reach only three-eights of an inch. They are light yellow or light brown.

A sharp sting

When attacking, the scorpion brings its tail up over its back. It can move its stinger in all directions except backward. And it stings quickly and repeatedly.

All scorpions have two saclike *venom glands*. The glands are connected to the stinger. Canals from the glands go to a small opening on the side of the stinger near the tip.

The strength of a scorpion's *venom* varies with each

The scorpion's sharp stinger is at the end of its tail. The scorpion raises its tail up over its head when attacking.

Venom slowly drips from the stinger of a desert scorpion.

species of scorpion. Scorpions that are harmful to mammals and humans belong to the *Buthidae* family. There are five other families of scorpions. The venom from these scorpions can be painful but not fatal to humans.

Not all animals react the same way to scorpion venom. Some species of frogs don't react at all. Porcupines, chickens, turkeys, toads, and cats react very little. All scorpion venom is harmful to insects.

Scientists know several ways to release the venom from a scorpion. One way is to place an electrified tweezer behind the venom glands. The electrical current causes the muscle to contract and release the venom. The drops are collected in a vial. Then the venom is frozen, or freeze dried.

Scientists hope to make better chemicals to kill insects by studying scorpion venom. These chemicals are called *insecticides*. Scientist also hope to make better *anti-serum* to help people who have been stung by studying scorpion venom.

Catching their prey

A scorpion's stinger and venom are its main survival tools. Without these powerful weapons, the scorpion would not live.

Scorpions are slow, and they don't see very well. To catch their food at night, they "listen" for vibrations from their prey with their legs and feet. They also surprise their prey. Scientists call this *ambush hunting*.

When a scorpion is resting, it lies on the ground with its tail to one side. When it hunts, it stands up. It opens its menacing front claws. The deadly stinger on the end of its tail is pointed forward. A slow moth or insect is about to become a meal.

When the scorpion senses prey, it grabs with its claws. If the victim struggles, the scorpion stings it. The scorpion's poison paralyzes its prey quickly. Only a small amount of venom is needed. The scorpion knows just

how to sting its prey so the poison will travel quickly to the nervous system.

When the prey stops wiggling, the scorpion holds it in its pincers. The soft insides of the victim are sucked into the scorpion's mouth.

As the scorpion feeds, it releases a digestive fluid on its prey. This fluid has *enzymes* that turn the prey into liquid. This is the only way the scorpion can eat its food. The scorpion begins to digest its food before it eats it.

Sometimes scorpions eat other scorpions. This happens only when food is scarce and there are too many scorpions. Usually scorpions like soft-bodied insects and occasionally a mouse or lizard.

Listening with their legs

Several years ago, scientists studied the sand scorpion in the Mojave Desert. They wanted to know how this scorpion found its prey.

A scientist had noticed a moth flying around a lantern at night. When the moth touched the sand near a scorpion, the scorpion quickly turned toward it and captured it. But if the scientist held a moth in the air over the scorpion, the scorpion didn't even know the moth was there.

Scientists knew the scorpion couldn't hear the moth. They also knew that it probably couldn't see its prey ei-

A Kenyan scorpion releases its digestive fluids onto a cricket before eating it.

ther. More tests were needed to figure out how the scorpion knew the moth was there.

The scientists watched the sand scorpion at night. They used ultraviolet light. In this type of light, the scorpion glowed in the dark and could be seen from up to 30 feet away.

They discovered that the scorpion could feel vibrations in the sand from the moth a foot away. The scorpion often caught a moth on its first try from a distance of four inches.

After more tests, the scientists realized that the scorpion was picking up vibrations with its feet—the only part of its body touching the ground. They also noticed that to make an accurate strike, the scorpion had to have all four pairs of feet on the ground at once.

The scientists examined the hairs on the scorpion's legs near the claws. These hairs had nerves that told the scorpion from where the vibrations in the sand were coming.

The scientists also discovered hairs on the feet of the scorpion that also pick up vibrations. In a sense, scorpions "listen" with the hairs on their legs and feet.

Some scorpions also make sounds of their own. *Palamnaeus swammerdami*, a scorpion that lives in India, makes a noise when it is frightened or angry. It sounds like a fingernail being pulled over the tips of a fine-tooth comb. This scorpion makes the sound by rubbing its arm against one of its front legs. Other scorpions do it the other way around. They rub their front legs against their arms.

14

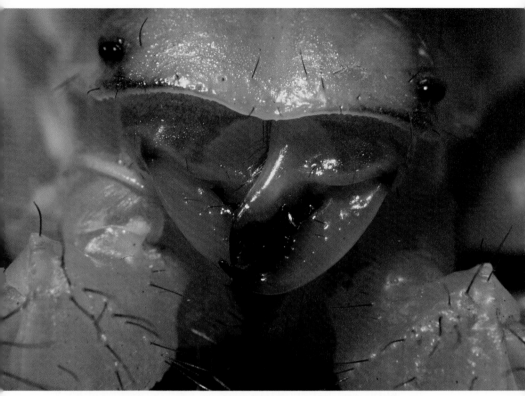

Tiny hairs around the giant scorpion's legs pick up vibrations in the ground and tell the scorpion if another animal is approaching.

Scorpions don't hear. At least, scientists can't find evidence that they do. Perhaps the sounds they make are used to frighten away enemies. But their sounds don't frighten monkeys or baboons. Scorpions are their favorite food. Monkeys and baboons are smart enough to pull off the stinger and claws before they eat a scorpion.

CHAPTER TWO:

Much to do about mating

For years, scientists have been watching scorpions mate. They have discovered that scorpions perform a courtship dance or walk. This is called the "promenade a deux," or "dance of two."

Jean Henri Fabre, a French scientist, named the dance. Fabre spent most of his life observing insects. When he was 80 years old, he studied the scorpion. Fabre studied the scorpions at night by holding a flashlight over cages of scorpions.

The mating of two scorpions begins when a male finds a female and grabs her arms with his claws. They dance forward and backward. Scientists believe scorpions do this to find the right place in which to mate. The dancing may go on for several hours with an occasional break for a rest. When they find a good place for mating, the scorpions sweep their abdomens and pectines along the ground. This creates a place for the male to deposit his *sperm* sac.

The male then drops a sperm sac onto the ground. The female pulls the sperm inside her genital opening. Once she has the sperm inside her, she frees herself from the

16

male's claws and pulls up her stinger. The male leaves and the female goes to her burrow. Within a week, the male can mate again.

Care of young

The fertilized eggs develop inside the female scorpion. When the young are born, they crawl forward toward the mother's mouth. She may eat a few, but the rest crawl up her arms to her back. It takes a few hours for all the young to get on her back. During this time, the mother doesn't feed them. They live off their own stored food.

At this stage, the young are really only *larvae*, or unde-

Newly hatched scorpions climb onto their mother's back and feed on food stored in their own bodies.

Once the young scorpions are on a female's back, they may completely cover her.

veloped scorpions. Their legs are short and do not have claws. The stingers on their short tails have no openings to release venom.

The mother may have 20 or more larvae on her back, completely hiding her body. Only her legs and tail can be seen.

After 10 to 16 days, the young change their entire skin.

This is their first molt. Afterward, they look like scorpions. They stay with the mother for a few more days. Then they leave to live on their own.

The young keep molting in order to grow. Each time, the old skin cracks open and is shed. This skin includes the lining of the *midgut, hindgut,* and the four pairs of book lungs. After a few days, the new outer shell has its final color.

Scorpions molt eight to ten times before they are full-size adults. This takes two to three years. Once they reach maturity, scorpions live another five to eight years.

After their first molt, the larvae look like adult scorpions and can live on their own.

This scorpion is found in the Sonoran Desert in southern Arizona.

CHAPTER THREE:

Most scorpions live in tropical or subtropical climates. Some species live in forests. Others live in fields and some in deserts. Some scorpions can adapt to different *habitats*. The forest scorpion, for instance, can live in the desert. And the desert scorpion can live in the forest.

20

There are about 56 species of scorpions in the United States. They can be found in at least three-fourths of the states. Arizona has 22 species. California and Florida also have many scorpion species. There are no scorpions in the New England states, Iowa, or in states around the Great Lakes however.

Scorpions also inhabit the European continent from

Thailand, in Southeast Asia, is the home of this scorpion.

The shaded areas show where scorpions can be found.

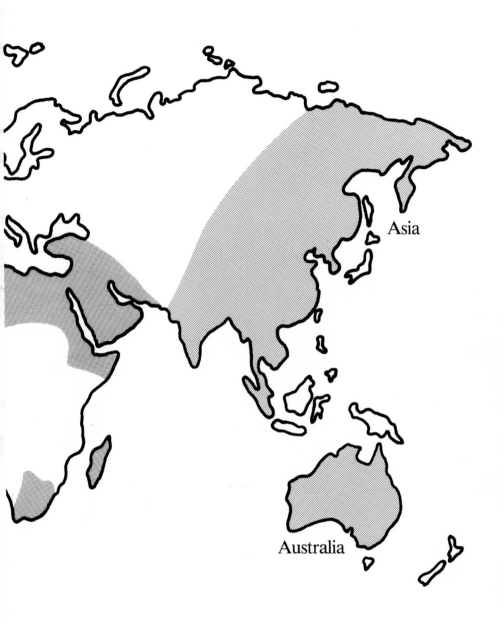

Asia

Australia

southern Germany to Mongolia and through most of Africa, Asia, and Australia. But they are not found on many islands. New Zealand, for instance, has no scorpions.

Living fossils

Scorpions are one of the oldest forms of life still found on the earth. Their basic form, body organization, and anatomy haven't changed in the last 300 million years. What you see today is what you would have seen 300 million years ago. Scorpions are referred to as "living fossils" because they have changed so little in all these years.

Scorpions originally lived in water. Scientists believe that water scorpions evolved into land scorpions.

They evolved because, over millions of years, great changes took place in the areas where scorpions lived. They had to adapt to stay alive. Areas that had been hot, became cold. Places that were cold, became hot. Wet areas grew dry and then wet again.

A scorpion had to adapt to its changing environment or die.

How scorpions live for so long

Scorpions have been able to survive heat and drought because many of them live underground. The climate un-

The basic form of the scorpion has not changed in 300 million years.

der the soil is protected from changes in the climate above ground.

Scorpions don't seem to need much food or water to stay alive. They can be kept at freezing temperatures for a week. When unfrozen, they return to normal in a few hours. They can survive underwater for days. Seven out of their eight book lungs can be blocked for long periods of time, and they will live. They don't need much air. Their movements are slow, so they don't need much energy to keep going. They can eat large amounts of food in a short time and then not eat for months. Some scorpions can live without eating for a year.

Scientists believe that only scorpion venom glands have changed over the years. For instance, if a scorpion lived in an area filled with cockroaches, then that scorpion developed a venom that was good for killing cockroaches.

Scorpions everywhere

Scorpions like to live where people live. They can be found in kitchens or under newspaper stored in dark places. They can be found in linen closets, under beds, or in shoes, couches, or clothing. They live in gardens and cellars, under logs and rocks, and in chicken houses and sandboxes. Even new buildings can be homes for scorpions, especially if they are close to old buildings.

This scorpion, found in Los Angeles, gets ready to strike.

When the temperature and soil conditions are right for scorpions to breed, large numbers can live in one place. Young scorpions stay close to where they were born. This creates what scientists call a *scorpion district*.

Several of these scorpion districts developed in small towns in Brazil between 1949 and 1963. About 138,500 scorpions were captured or killed in these towns. All of them were the genus and species *Tityus serrulatus*, one of the scorpions most poisonous to humans. When insecticides were used in these towns, buckets of dead scorpions were swept off the streets.

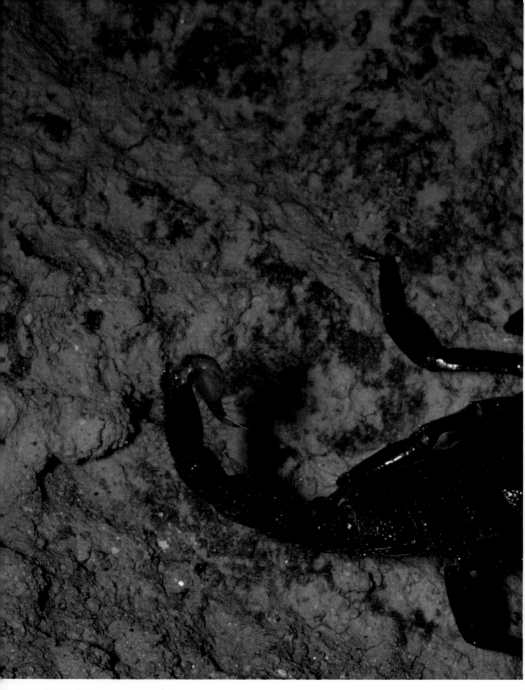

One of the many scorpion species found in India.

The bark scorpion is found mainly in Arizona.

CHAPTER FOUR:

The Buthidae family

The most important family of scorpions is the Buthidae. Half of all scorpion species, and all the scorpions that are poisonous to people, belong to this family.

The slender scorpion or bark scorpion (*Centruroides*

sculpturatus) in the Buthidae family is the only species in the United States that is poisonous to humans. It lives mainly in Arizona but can also be found in New Mexico, Texas, and California. Some live in the Grand Canyon.

The slender scorpion is straw colored and only one half to three inches long. The segments of its tail are oblong rather than square. Forty to sixty people are treated for slender scorpion bites in Arizona each year.

The giant hairy scorpion (*Hadrurus spadix*) also lives in Arizona, but its venom is not dangerous to humans. The giant hairy scorpion is five and a half inches long. Insects are its main food, but it also eats lizards and small snakes.

The common yellow scorpion (*Buthus occitanus*),

The venom of the giant hairy scorpion is not poisonous to humans.

found throughout France, is poisonous to people. The yellow scorpion that lives in southern France can produce eight milligrams of poison at one time. The yellow scorpion that lives in North Africa is even more dangerous to people than its relative in southern France.

Another North African scorpion, the fat-tailed scorpion (*Androctonus australis*), is three to four inches long.

The North African yellow scorpion is one of the most dangerous scorpions.

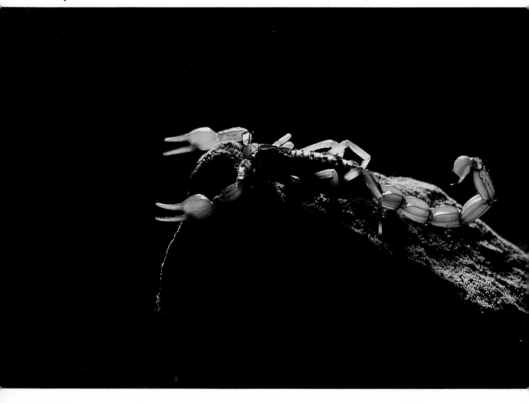

This species has adapted well to its dry climate. When necessary, it can go without food for six months. The venom from the fat-tailed scorpion is almost as poisonous as the venom from a cobra. It has killed a dog in seven minutes and a human in four hours.

A scorpion living in the United States that is not poisonous to people is *Centruroides vittatus*. It can be found in Georgia, Florida, Kansas, Texas, Arkansas, Louisiana, New Mexico, and South Carolina. The sting from this scorpion causes a sharp pain that swells but soon disappears.

The Durango scorpion (*Centruroidos suffusus*) is found in Durango, Mexico. The sting from this scorpion is often fatal to children under the age of seven.

Some scientists believe that the sting from *Tityus serrulates* is the most dangerous to humans. This scorpion ranges from yellowish to blackish brown and lives in Brazil.

A large scorpion living in the forest of the the Philippines is the *Palamnaeus longimanus*. It lives under decaying logs and in holes of dead trees. Compared to most scorpions, it drinks large amounts of water. It very seldom uses its stinger to kill its prey.

CHAPTER FIVE:

What a scorpion sting does

There are two kinds of scorpion stings. One can hardly be noticed. It may hurt for an hour or two, but that is all. The second kind is deadly. It poisons a victim's whole system.

Scorpions usually sting human beings accidentally—the scorpion is surprised and stings to protect itself. Scorpions sting people more often at night, when scorpions are active. They also sting more frequently when the weather is hot and stormy.

Most people are stung in houses or tents, or while they are gardening. Adults are stung about as often as children, but the venom makes children much sicker. People are usually stung on their legs or arms.

What happens when someone is stung by a poisonous scorpion? At first, the sting is painful. If a finger is stung, the whole arm will hurt. The pain is replaced soon by a feeling of numbness. Then the victim quickly becomes tense and nervous. Sometimes he or she cannot stand still. *Sedatives* don't seem to help. Muscles begin to twitch. The tongue seems thick, and the person cannot talk. The victim sneezes over and over again. Saliva flows from the

34

A scorpion sting can be lethal to small animals. Here, a Kenyan scorpion has stung and killed a small mouse.

mouth. The heart rate increases. The eyes tear. Sweat pours off the body. Young children begin to convulse. Sometimes adults also go into convulsions. Breathing becomes irregular.

Vomiting is the first sign that nerve centers have been attacked by the venom. This is a bad sign. Most people who begin to vomit do not survive. They die because their breathing, or respiratory system, is paralyzed.

Some scorpion stings, like the one from the brown centruroides, can be painful to humans.

36

The first symptoms may occur within five minutes to twenty-four hours after the sting. Most often they appear sometime between twenty minutes and four hours. But a person can die from a sting in two hours.

A victim must be watched for a least twelve hours after the last symptoms have stopped. Often relapses happen. Victims have been known to stop breathing after they have been fine for hours.

People who recover often find that the area around the sting stays sore for a few days.

How to avoid scorpion stings

Scorpion stings can be frightening, but fear of them shouldn't stop you from having fun when you go camping or exploring. After all, you can probably avoid scorpion stings by taking certain precautions. When camping in scorpion territory, you can be especially careful about looking for scorpions in your bedding, clothes, and shoes. Shake out shoes before putting them on. Shake clothing out, too. Check your sleeping bag before climbing inside. In the morning, roll it up. Put it someplace off the ground so scorpions can't climb into it.

People who live in scorpion territory can be careful about not piling lumber or rocks near their homes. These are places where scorpions might hide. When moving piles of anything outside, it is wise to wear gloves.

You can also make the outside of the house near the ground scorpionproof. This can be done by using slippery surfaces like ceramic tile. Scorpions can't climb smooth surfaces. Spraying with insecticide around the outside of the house can keep scorpions from coming in, too.

Inside the house, baseboards and cracks also can be sprayed. Attics and cellars, where scorpions often live,

Scorpions like to hide under rocks and beneath lumber.

should be sprayed, too. Remember that when the attic heats to over 100 degrees, scorpions search for cooler air in the house. So other areas may need to be treated as well.

It is also important to eliminate cockroaches and any other prey that scorpions like to eat.

What to do if you are stung

Learning what to do in case you or someone you are with is stung can calm fears. The most important thing is to treat each sting as potentially dangerous, even though most aren't. The victim should be taken to a hospital immediately. If possible, also bring the scorpion that caused the sting. Then the doctor will know what kind of anti-serum to use. Children should always be treated with anti-serum.

Scorpion anti-serum is generally available in places where dangerous scorpions live. There are different serums for different scorpions, so make sure the right one is used.

If no medical help is available, someone with first aid training can place a tourniquet above the sting, make a light cut over the sting, and suck on it to remove the poison.

Antihistamines, or allergy drugs, only ease symptoms.

Scorpions can climb rough surfaces to get into houses. People who live in scorpion territory often surround their houses with smooth materials, like tile, to prevent scorpions from climbing in.

They do not counteract the poison. Sometimes artificial respiration can help if the respiratory system stops.

For a serious scorpion sting, the best course is rapid medical help and a dose of anti-serum. The patient must be watched until out of danger.

How to keep a scorpion as a pet

Most people go to so much trouble to avoid scorpions that you might think no one would ever want one as a pet. But some people do.

Some specialized pet shops sell scorpions. The buyer has to be over 18 years old or have parental approval. The usual cost is between $19 and $35 per pet.

The best place to keep a scorpion is in a glass *terrarium*, which scorpions cannot climb out of. The bottom of the terrarium should be covered with sand and a "hot rock" placed inside. This rock that is kept warm by electrical current will keep the temperature in the cage at 80 to 85 degrees Fahrenheit. The scorpion will also need to have something to crawl under, along with a dish or wet sponge for drinking water.

Cactus plants should not be put in the cage. The sharp spines of the cactus plant can hurt a scorpion.

Pet shops usually sell food for scorpions. The food, like fly larva, crickets, and small mice, should be alive. It is better to have only one scorpion at a time because the animals do occasionally eat each other.

Scorpions can be dangerous. But if you are careful, you can avoid ever being stung by one. You may just decide to keep one as a pet.

When feeding a pet scorpion, keep in mind that a scorpion likes to kill its own prey.

Although some scorpion stings are harmful to humans, precautions can be taken to insure that a scorpion will not become startled and attack.

44

INDEX/GLOSSARY:

46

INDEX/GLOSSARY:

to pick up prey.

PREY 8, 11, 13, 33, 41—*An animal that is hunted for food by other animals.*

SCORPION DISTRICT 27—*An area in which a large number of scorpions are living.*

SCORPIONIDA 5—*The order to which scorpions belong.*

SEDATIVES 34—*Medications that tend to calm, moderate, or tranquilize nervousness or excitement.*

SPECIES 8, 20, 21, 27, 30, 31, 33—*A group of animals or plants with common features that set it apart from other groups.*

SPERM 16—*Fluid produced by a male that must combine with a female's egg to produce young.*

SPIRACLES 8—*Four pairs of openings on the underside of the scorpion that bring air into the book lungs.*

TERRARIUM 42—*An enclosure with glass sides used to raise small animals.*

VENOM 8, 10, 11, 18, 26, 33, 34, 35—*Poison released through the scorpion's stinger.*

VENOM GLANDS 8, 10, 26—*Two saclike structures near a scorpion's stinger that produce venom.*